ROBERT MUCZYNSK
DUOS FOR FLUTE
AND CLARINET

Flute and Clarinet in B♭

ED-3840

ISBN 978-0-7935-0970-6

G. SCHIRMER, Inc.

DISTRIBUTED BY

HAL•LEONARD®
CORPORATION
7777 W. BLUEMOUND RD. P.O. BOX 13819 MILWAUKEE, WI 53213

recording: Laurel Record, LR131, Julius Baker, Flute, Mitchell Lurie, Clarinet

This work is also available in a version for two flutes, HL50291720

to the memory of Camil Van Hulse

DUOS FOR FLUTE AND CLARINET

I

Robert Muczynski
Op. 24

II

Allegro risoluto

III

Moderato

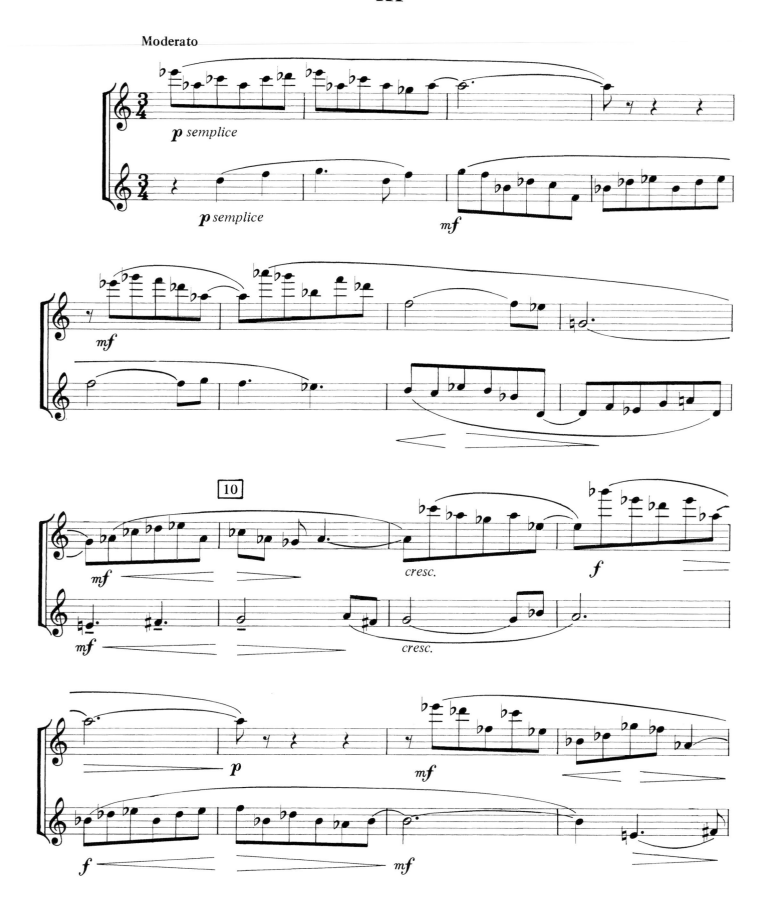

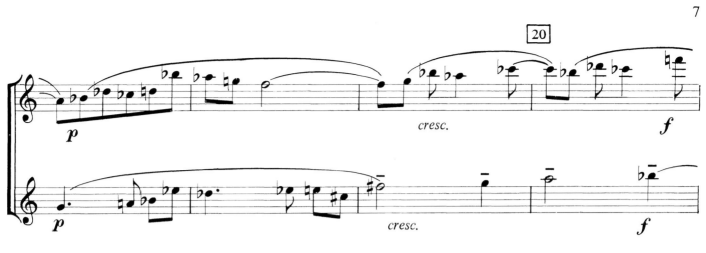

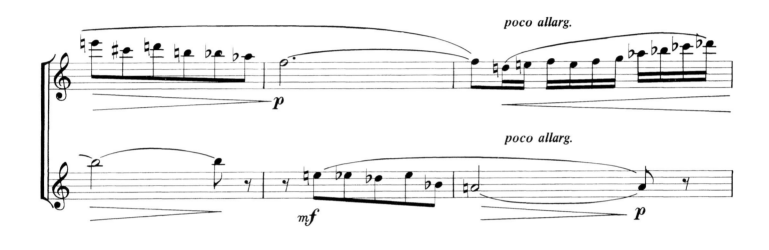

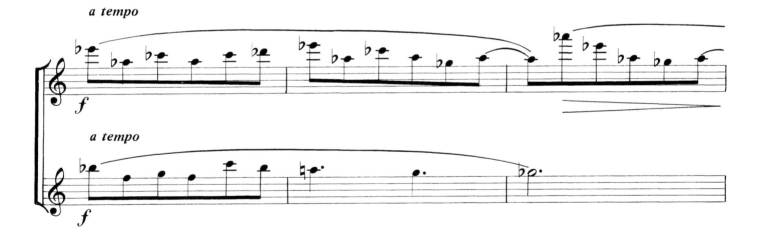

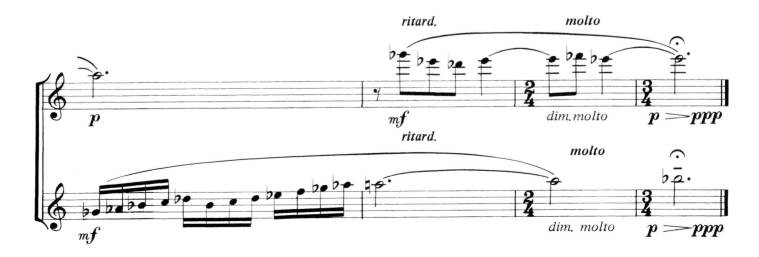

IV

Allegro ma non troppo

V

VI

ROBERT MUCZYNSKI
DUOS FOR FLUTE AND CLARINET

Flute and Clarinet in B♭

ED-3840

ISBN 978-0-7935-0970-6

G. SCHIRMER, Inc.

DISTRIBUTED BY

HAL•LEONARD®
CORPORATION
7777 W. BLUEMOUND RD. P.O. BOX 13819 MILWAUKEE, WI 53213

recording: Laurel Record, LR131, Julius Baker, Flute, Mitchell Lurie, Clarinet

This work is also available in a version for two flutes, HL50291720

to the memory of Camil Van Hulse

DUOS FOR FLUTE AND CLARINET

I

Robert Muczynski
Op. 24

II

Allegro risoluto

III

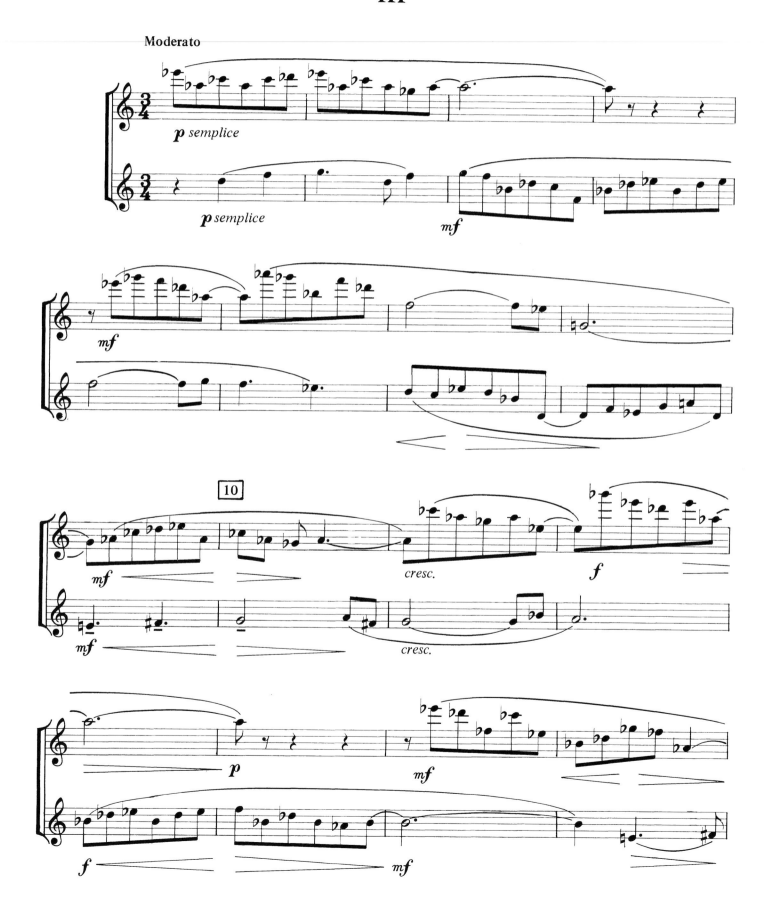

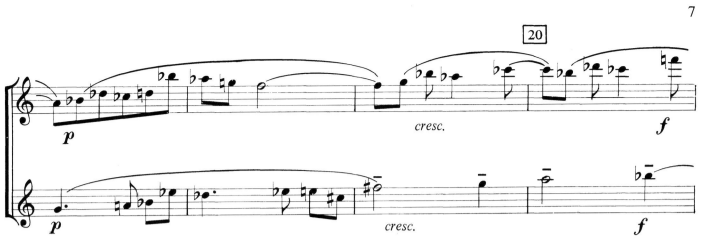

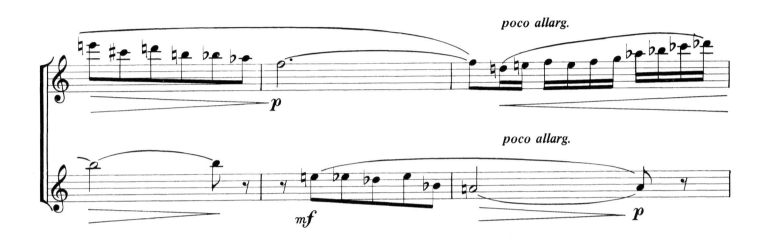

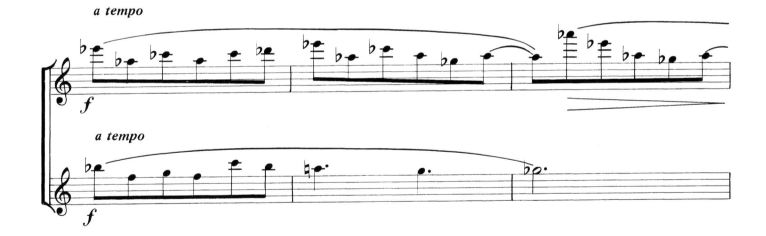

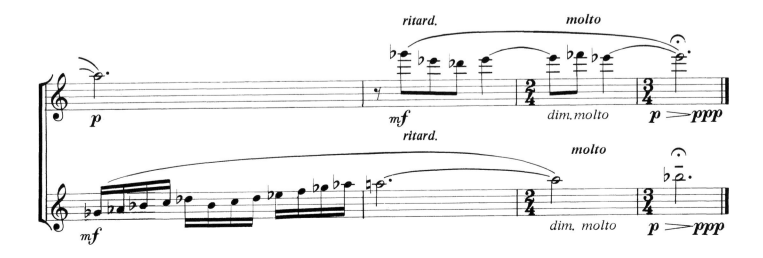

IV

V

VI